Jiggelo

Jiggelo

inventive gelatin shots
for creative imbibers

Mary Breidenbach, Barrett J. Calhoon, & Sharon L. Calhoon

TEN SPEED PRESS
www.tenspeed.com

1☺

Ten Speed Press
P.O. Box 7123
Berkeley, California 94707
www.tenspeed.com

Distributed in Australia by Simon and Schuster Australia, in Canada by Ten Speed Press Canada, in New Zealand by Southern Publishers Group, in South Africa by Real Books, and in the United Kingdom and Europe by Airlift Book Company.

Cover and interior design by Mary Breidenbach
Jiggelo photography by Barrett J. Calhoon
Photograph on cover © The Image Bank/Getty Images
Images on pages 23, 38, 89, and 90 courtesy Retro Ad Art ©1997 AdGraphics
Photograph on page 45 © MODIS Land Rapid Response Team, NASA/GSFC, http://visibleearth.nasa.gov/

Images from private collections are noted on page 90. All uncredited images are from unknown sources or by unknown photographers. Every effort has been made to trace accurate ownership of copyrighted visual material used in this book. Errors or omissions will be corrected in subsequent editions, provided notification is sent to the publisher.

Library of Congress Cataloging-in-Publication Data:

Breidenbach, Mary.
  Jiggelo inventive gelatin shots for creative imbibers / Mary Breidenbach, Barrett J. Calhoon, and Sharon L. Calhoon.
      p. cm.
  Includes index.
  ISBN 1-58008-596-2
  1. Cookery (Gelatin) 2. Cocktails. I. Calhoon, Barrett J. II. Calhoon, Sharon L. III. Title.
  TX814.5.G4B74 2004
  641.8'642—dc22
                                                                    2004000620

First printing, 2004
Printed in Hong Kong

1 2 3 4 5 6 7 8 9 10 — 08 07 06 05 04

Contents

Introduction

Gelatin shots have evolved from youth-oriented novelty drinks to multigenerational trendy cocktails. Creative imbibers thought outside the vodka-and-gelatin box, and a universe of inventive shots unfolded.

Perhaps you recall when your basic food groups were Captain Crunch, NyQuil, and gelatin shots, and your kitchenette essentials were one spoon and a chipped mug. Maybe that was last week. Then the day came when you realized that you owned a whisk and that what used to be your larder of beer and vodka had become a collection of gins, rums, and wines. Finally, you have found your place in the Jiggelo Generation—one foot in the innovation of youthful consumption and the other in the unfathomable potential of adult partaking.

Jiggelology

Fortunately, there aren't a lot of rules, procedures, or mathematical laws involved in the jiggelo creation process, and no stemware is required. There is, however, a lot of room for creativity—and you can usually drink your mistakes.

Heating: You may use a stove, microwave, or Bunsen burner to bring required liquids to a boil.

Container: Any heat-resistant (nonmelting) bowl or container that will hold all the liquid can be used. A 2-cup Pyrex measuring cup is useful but not mandatory.

Measuring: A measuring cup and set of measuring spoons will be needed.

Mixing: A whisk, or fork, is the best utensil to incorporate the gelatin into the liquid. Unless you are not responsible for clean up, we recommend you do not use froth-and-splatter-producing electric mixers or blenders. Always stir the hot liquid and gelatin until the powder is completely dissolved. This is especially important when using unflavored gelatin.

Flavored Gelatin: Use your favorite brand of gelatin. Sugar-free and some vegetarian gelatins may be substituted in these recipes.

Unflavored Gelatin: Remember when you went from printing to cursive and felt so mature having found another way to express yourself? Well, it's kind of like that when you discover the versatility of unflavored gelatin. These recipes are created for success, and you'll feel empowered after preparing just a few!

Unflavored gelatin (alternatively spelled *gelatine*) also has no sweetener or coloring. There are usually four little packages, or envelopes, in a small box of gelatin. Although they are not usually labeled by weight, each envelope contains .25 ounce of gelatin.

Most gelatin box directions call for less liquid than these recipes. No worries. Jiggelo recipes have just the right amount of liquid to make a silky, satisfying texture.

Unflavored gelatin takes a little longer to dissolve. Use a whisk and be attentive to the recipe's directions. You will probably notice the liquid frothing as you whisk. This is normal. Do not leave the gelatin unattended while heating because it can quickly boil over.

If desired, you may add a few drops of food coloring.

Vegetarian Jiggelos: Neither flavored nor unflavored gelatin is vegetarian. Hain SuperFruits Vegetarian Dessert Mix (see Resources, page 88) may be substituted for most gelatin. Don't worry if the the mix is clumped in the package; it will incorporate into the hot liquid if whisked for about 2 minutes. Make sure all liquids you add are at room temperature. The mixture will set quickly, so stir frequently as you pour the jiggelos into cups. You may find you have to reduce the amount of liquid to achieve desired firmness.

Liquor: The general rule is: If you wouldn't drink it alone, you shouldn't use it in a jiggelo. If you don't like gin, you probably won't like a gin-based jiggelo. Also, use the quality of liquor you enjoy drinking. Cream-based liqueurs, such as Bailey's, KeKe Beach, and Tequila Rose, tend to separate. This may look different (sometimes even attractive), but it will not affect the taste of the shot. Also, make sure you keep those creamy liqueurs refrigerated after opening.

Milk: When a jiggelo calls for milk, you may use any kind you wish. Jiggelos have been successfully tested with soy milk, lactose-free milk, and all varieties of homogenized milks. Whole milk will make your jiggelos creamier.

Flattened Soda: Some jiggelos call for flattened soda. To achieve the desired flatness, pour the soda into a cup and cover loosely with a cloth or paper towel. Let sit for 4 hours, stirring occasionally.

Distribution: Any ladle, cup, or pitcher that pours easily may be used. Use a turkey baster for clean, evenly layered shots.

Containment: Unless otherwise indicated, the instructions call for, and we highly recommend, disposable 1-ounce cups.

Also referred to as soufflé cups, they are available at restaurant supply stores and online (see Resources, page 88). They're ideal because you can fill them to the top giving you attractive jiggelos of consistent volume. Additionally, most soufflé cups are translucent, enabling views of dramatic colors and/or submerged embellishments. These cups come in an assortment of shapes, and lids may also be purchased to make transporting a breeze. One-ounce servings allow people to try several different jiggelos responsibly. They are affordable and easy to use.

Alternative Containment: Plastic 3-ounce cups available at most groceries are the most readily available disposable containers. If you use these cups, please do not fill them more than half full if you are planning multiple servings for each person. Ice cube trays and rubber molds are other options. Spraying them lightly with cooking spray prior to filling will help them release easily. You may also pour jiggelo liquid into pre-sprayed baking pans and cut them into cubes after they are firm. Some jiggelos beg to be created in edible chocolate cups (see Resources, page 88). Or you may want to experiment with small hollowed-out fruits such as kumquats or apricots as edible containers. Finally, clear shot glasses or small, stemmed cocktail glasses filled with nicely garnished jiggelos look particularly classy and are environmentally friendly. Of course, the number of servings will vary if the serving size fluctuates from 1 ounce.

Hazardous Containment: Avoid the use of paper cups. Because warm liquid can make the seams weaken, all your tasty jiggelo effort will seep out.

Trays: Use a tray, cookie sheet, or cake pan lined with a paper towel to set your jiggelos in before you refrigerate them. Trays can be stacked.

Refrigeration: The time needed for jiggelos to become firm varies with the refrigerator, the temperature of the liquid, and the alcohol content. Allow several hours. Most jiggelos are best consumed within 24 hours of creation, though they will keep for up to 3 days in the refrigerator if covered.

Yields: The recipe yields are based on 1-ounce serving sizes. Recipes may be easily multiplied for large parties.

Jiggelo Time Line

1682	A Frenchman named Papin creates gelatin.
1845	Peter Cooper obtains the first patent for gelatin dessert.
1897	Pearle and May Davis, of LeRoy, New York, create four fruit flavored gelatins and name the products Jell-O.
1904	The first Jell-O recipe book appears, as well as an ad campaign claiming, "You can't be a child without it."
early 20th c.	Immigrants are welcomed to Ellis Island with servings of Jell-O.
1944	Publication of *Bright Spots of Wartime Meals—66 Ration-Wise Recipes* encourages the use of Jell-O as a food expander.
1962	A Bakersfield, California, housewife discovers that secretly substituting some vodka for water in her strawberry gelatin mellows out her entire family.
1976	An All-American imbibing tradition takes root when a state college frat boy creates a tubful of orange gelatin spiked with Everclear.
1994	Guards confiscate gelatin shots from Parrot Heads entering a Jimmy Buffet concert in Detroit, Michigan.
2002	Four friends creatively imbibe around a table in Indianapolis, Indiana, while discussing the current, increasingly complex status of the once humble gelatin shot. Jiggelo is born.

BE SMART, STAY SMART.
Consume all alcoholic beverages responsibly and safely.

Jiggelo Savvy

- It can sometimes be difficult to find small (3-ounce) boxes of the flavor gelatin you desire. A large (6-ounce) box can be divided in half. Five tablespoons of flavored, sweetened gelatin equals a 3-ounce box. If you'd like to use unsweetened gelatin, substitute $2\frac{1}{2}$ teaspoons for one 3-ounce box.

- Using little sample liquor bottles can save you dollars and space. A 50-ml bottle of liquor is equal to $\frac{1}{4}$ cup or 4 tablespoons.

- One-ounce disposable cups can be easily transported in pizza boxes!

- Jiggelos love company. Make sure to have some food and nonalcoholic beverages available when serving jiggelos.

Measurement Conversions

3 teaspoons = 1 tablespoon
2 tablespoons = 1 fluid ounce
2 tablespoons = $\frac{1}{8}$ cup
4 tablespoons = $\frac{1}{4}$ cup
5 tablespoons + 1 teaspoon = $\frac{1}{3}$ cup
8 tablespoons = $\frac{1}{2}$ cup
$\frac{1}{4}$ cup = 2 fluid ounces
$\frac{1}{4}$ cup = 50 ml

Doing Jiggelos

Some noted ways to do a jiggelo and their nonverbal implications:

The Spooner: Dig in with a spoon.
Note: Tighty whities.

The Implement Rimmer: Insert an implement, such as a toothpick, pretzel stick, or table knife, between the jiggelo and the cup. Move the implement around the side of the gelatin, separating it from the container. Squeeze the bottom of the cup and slurp the jiggelo into your mouth.
Note: Method of the fastidious and accommodating.

The Squeezer: Squeeze the bottom of the jiggelo container, forcing the contents to break up and mound outward, thus enabling sucking and slurping into the mouth.
Note: Technique of the self-conscious and tentative.

The Finger Rimmer: Same as the Implement Rimmer except using an extended finger.
Note: Those who lick or suck their finger after rimming are hotties.

The Tongue Rimmer: Same as above but use your extended tongue rather than a finger.
Note: Tongue Rimmers are last to be voted off the island.

The Ripper: If container permits, rip it away from the shot, eviscerating the container and bare-handedly devouring the jiggelo.
Note: Seduction is not in Ripper's vocabulary; immediate gratification is.

Alliteration
Peter Blow
Need
Jungle Juice
Cram
Newton's Headache
Haze

Chapter 1
Old School

Your group imbibing experiences may never reach the heights they achieved during your college days in terms of both frequency and magnitude. But you can try. Old School means any excuse and open invitations. When spirited people assemble, jiggelos are mandatory, often making the difference between a pass or fail party.

Alliteration

There once was a lovely Lolita,
who loved levitating lemon gelitas.
They'd rise in the air,
fall mouth-bound with flair,
lavish lip-licking Latina Jiggelita.

1 (3-ounce) package lemon gelatin
1 cup water
½ cup citron vodka
½ cup lemoncello

Place the gelatin in a heat-resistant bowl. Bring the water to a boil. Pour the water over the gelatin, stirring until dissolved. Add the citron vodka and lemoncello, mixing well. Divide the mixture among 20 disposable 1-ounce cups. Chill in the refrigerator until firm, 2 to 4 hours.

Makes 20 jiggelos

"Enormous! They must weigh 10 kilos each!"
—Lupe Ontiveros as Carmen in *Real Women Have Curves*

Jungle Juice

Remember when the recipe for a party was sixty of your closest friends and the random bottles of booze they brought mixed in a tub with fruit punch? Jungle Juice! Recreate the madness with this irreverent jiggelo. Quadruple the recipe and add friends.

1 ¼ cups cold fruit punch
1 envelope unflavored gelatin
4 tablespoons vodka
4 tablespoons rum
4 tablespoons tequila
1 (3.5-ounce) can fruit cocktail, drained
**   (optional)**

Hank: "What's that?"
Josh: "It's a math award."
Hank: "Looks like a dildo."
—Mark Carapezza as Hank and Tom Everett Scott
  as Josh in *Dead Man on Campus*

Pour the cold fruit punch into a small sauce pan and sprinkle with gelatin. Whisk the mixture well, then let it sit for 3 minutes. Place the pan over medium heat and bring the mixture to a boil, whisking frequently to ensure the gelatin dissolves. Immediately remove the pan from the heat and let the mixture cool for 10 minutes. Add the vodka, rum, and tequila, mixing well. Divide the mixture among 18 disposable 1-ounce cups, leaving ¹/₂ inch of space at the top if using the fruit cocktail. Add one or two pieces of the fruit cocktail to each cup. Chill in the refrigerator until firm, 2 to 4 hours.

Makes 18 jiggelos

Cram

Would you really want to be friends with someone who had never ever crammed for an exam? There's a bit of slacker in the best of us. Just as cramming is an educational survival strategy, this cranberry jiggelo is a celebration of cramming survival.

1 (3-ounce) package cranberry gelatin
1 cup water
½ cup Southern Comfort
½ cup citron vodka

Place the gelatin in a heat-resistant bowl. Bring the water to a boil. Pour the water over the gelatin, stirring until dissolved. Add the Southern Comfort and citron vodka, mixing well. Divide the mixture among 20 disposable 1-ounce cups. Chill in the refrigerator until firm, 2 to 4 hours.

Makes 20 jiggelos

"Why is it that the good old American slacker gets no respect for his detachment, but hey, the Buddhist monk does?"
—Donal Logue as Dex in *The Tao of Steve*

Newton's Headache

Coincidence? In 1682, the very year England's Sir Isaac Newton observed Halley's comet and worked on theories of universal gravitation, a Frenchman named Papin created the substance we now call gelatin. Celebrate the international collision of history-altering breakthroughs with this apple-cinnamon jiggelo.

- 1 cup cold water
- 1 envelope unflavored gelatin
- $\frac{1}{3}$ cup apple juice concentrate
- $\frac{1}{3}$ cup Apple Pucker
- $\frac{1}{4}$ cup hard cider
- 2 tablespoons Goldschläger

Pour the cold water in a small sauce pan and sprinkle with the gelatin. Whisk the mixture well, then let it sit for 3 minutes. Place the pan over medium heat and bring the mixture to a boil, whisking frequently to ensure the gelatin dissolves. Immediately remove the pan from the heat and let the mixture cool for 10 minutes. Add the apple juice concentrate, Apple Pucker, hard cider, and Goldschläger, mixing well. Divide the mixture among 16 to 18 disposable 1-ounce cups. Chill in the refrigerator until firm, 2 to 4 hours.

Makes 16 to 18 jiggelos

"I feign no hypotheses."
—Sir Isaac Newton,
Principia Mathematica

Haze

This is one mean jiggelo. Seriously, it will throw a look on your face reminiscent of a debutant eating hissing cockroaches. Partake for the genuine, hard driving, college-haze flash back. Please proceed with caution.

1 (3-ounce) package cherry gelatin
1 ¹/₂ cups water
¹/₂ cup Everclear
1 tablespoon ouzo or Jägermeister

Place the gelatin in a heat-resistant bowl. Bring the water to a boil. Pour the water over the gelatin, stirring until dissolved. Add the Everclear and ouzo, mixing well. Divide the mixture among 20 disposable 1-ounce cups. Chill in the refrigerator until firm, 2 to 4 hours.

Makes 20 jiggelos

Jiggel the Night Astray

Barry Baron and the Jiggel-Dees

Angela: "Do you trust him?"
Dr. Champion: "Yeah. I used to hold him over
the toilet at frat parties."
—Sandra Bullock as Angela Bennett and Dennis Miller
as Dr. Alan Champion in *The Net*

ISO Gainful Employment
ISO Balance
ISO ISP
ISO Ms. Right
ISO Mr. Right
ISO Alternatives
ISO Happy Endings

Chapter 2

In Search Of . . .

Even "in-betweens" should be acknowledged and celebrated, particularly the in-betweeness of searching. Jobs, dates, ISPs, IPOs, mates— gather fellow seekers and quench your quest with ISO jiggelos.

ISOGainful Employment

Ten million Americans search for jobs annually. Daunting? Exciting? Either way, kick back and taste the green-green of this jiggelo while pondering the creative embellishments of your resume. No cover letter required.

1 (3-ounce) package lime gelatin
¾ cup water
½ cup citron vodka
½ cup gin
¼ cup Rose's Sweetened Lime Juice

Place the gelatin in a heat-resistant bowl. Bring the water to a boil. Pour the water over the gelatin, stirring until dissolved. Add the citron vodka, gin, and Rose's Sweetened Lime Juice, mixing well. Divide the mixture among 20 disposable 1-ounce cups. Chill in the refrigerator until firm, 2 to 4 hours.

Makes 20 jiggelos

"Graduation was just two days away, and I couldn't wait to get started on that wife and kids and pension plan thing."
—Ben Affleck as Jack in *Glory Daze*

ISOBalance

So much to balance, so little time. The balance of work and play. The balance of consumerism and nonmaterialism. The balance of inner peace. And the balance of the checkbook. Most forms of balance are as fleeting as these delicious and tipsy jiggelos will be at your next party.

1 (3-ounce) package watermelon gelatin
1 cup water
¹/₂ cup Midori
¹/₄ cup raspberry vodka
¹/₄ cup peach schnapps

Place the gelatin in a heat-resistant bowl. Bring the water to a boil. Pour the water over the gelatin, stirring until dissolved. Add the Midori, raspberry vodka, and peach schnapps, mixing well. Divide the mixture among 20 disposable 1-ounce cups. Chill in the refrigerator until firm, 2 to 4 hours.

Makes 20 jiggelos

"The truth is balance, but the opposite of truth, which is unbalance, may not be a lie."
—Susan Sontag, American writer and cultural critic with an impressive mane of hair

ISO ISP

A good Internet Service Provider, like a good friend, is hard to find. Both are fun, quick when you need them, and available 24-7, but at least good friends don't pop up and ask you to purchase Viagra constantly. This banana-rama jiggelo is a lot like a good friend, easier to acquire than a good ISP, and it satisfies without annoying.

1 (3-ounce) package strawberry-banana gelatin
1 cup water
1 cup banana rum
1 tablespoon Frangelico

Place the gelatin in a heat-resistant bowl. Bring the water to a boil. Pour the water over the gelatin, stirring until dissolved. Add the banana rum and Frangelico, mixing well. Divide the mixture among 20 disposable 1-ounce cups. Chill in the refrigerator until firm, 2 to 4 hours.

Makes 20 jiggelos

"Just what do you think you're doing, Dave? . . .
Look Dave, I can see you're really upset about this.
I honestly think you ought to sit down calmly,
take a stress pill, and think it over."
—Voice of Douglas Rain as HAL 9000 in *2001: A Space Odyssey*

ISO Ms. Right

We bet that one or two deliciously sensuous peach-raspberry jiggelos will be more effective than this personal ad: "LOVE HURTS. But I'll take another chance. DBM ISO tall, thin brunette. Cross between Salma, Katherine Zeta, and Halle. You: 23–28, mature, emotionally/financially stable, classy but casual, structured but spontaneous & desires to be spoiled."

1 (3-ounce) package peach gelatin
1 cup water
½ cup raspberry vodka
⅓ cup peach schnapps
2 tablespoons Chambord

Place the gelatin in a heat-resistant bowl. Bring the water to a boil. Pour the water over the gelatin, stirring until dissolved. Add the raspberry vodka, peach schnapps, and Chambord, mixing well. Divide the mixture among 20 disposable 1-ounce cups. Chill in the refrigerator until firm, 2 to 4 hours.

Makes 20 jiggelos

"I would probably begin with the very classy first line. Something like, 'Say sweet thing, can I buy you a fish sandwich?'"
—Tim Meadows as Leon Phelps in *The Ladies Man*

ISO Mr. Right

"PRETTY, FIT SWPF 5'6", 125, 20s ISO kind, fit, tall, young man. I'm fun loving, kind, with many interests. I love jiggelos! Are you Mr. Right?"

Now that you have his attention, capture him with this jiggelo that guys particularly love!

1 (3-ounce) package apricot gelatin or peach gelatin
1 cup water
¹/₂ cup Kentucky bourbon
¹/₂ cup vodka

Place the gelatin in a heat-resistant bowl. Bring the water to a boil. Pour the water over the gelatin, stirring until dissolved. Add the bourbon and vodka, mixing well. Divide the mixture among 20 disposable 1-ounce cups. Chill in the refrigerator until firm, 2 to 4 hours.

Makes 20 jiggelos

"Am I making believe I see in you a man too perfect to be really true? Do I want you because you're wonderful? Or are you wonderful because I want you?"
—Brandy singing as Cinderella in *Cinderella*

ISOAlternatives

"*PURPLE WAVES FROTH, be filled with lustrous lunar elixir. Couple with transvestite man ISO role-playing couple for passionate, intimate connection.*"

Every alternative adventure deserves a jiggelo, the alternative cocktail.

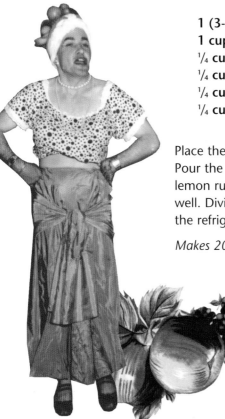

1 (3-ounce) package mixed fruit gelatin
1 cup water
$\frac{1}{4}$ cup lemon rum
$\frac{1}{4}$ cup vanilla vodka
$\frac{1}{4}$ cup apple vodka
$\frac{1}{4}$ cup peach schnapps

Place the gelatin in a heat-resistant bowl. Bring the water to a boil. Pour the water over the gelatin, stirring until dissolved. Add the lemon rum, vanilla vodka, apple vodka, and peach schnapps, mixing well. Divide the mixture among 20 disposable 1-ounce cups. Chill in the refrigerator until firm, 2 to 4 hours.

Makes 20 jiggelos

"*Your ad intrigued me, Soulmate. A little about myself: I love dressing up and getting down. I'm something of a walking contradiction—open minded yet lactose intolerant. And I yearn for someone who likes big surprises. Call me.*"
—Personals ad voice mail in *Buying the Cow*

ISOHappy Endings

Everyone swoons for this super popular jiggelo, and why not? It's everything a pretty woman loves and almost everything her man desires to give her. We advocate role-playing: the girls as slutty, spunky Vivian and the guys as uptight, rich Edward. Substitute ISO Happy Endings for champagne, and add strawberries and whipped cream for an aphrodisiacal effect.

1 (3-ounce) package wild strawberry or strawberry gelatin
³/₄ cup water
³/₄ cup champagne or Asti Spumante
¹/₂ cup crème de strawberry
20 fresh strawberries (optional)
1 (7-ounce) can whipped cream (optional)

Place the gelatin in a heat-resistant bowl. Bring the water to a boil. Pour the water over the gelatin, stirring until dissolved. Add the champagne and crème de strawberry, mixing well. Distribute the mixture among 20 disposable 1-ounce cups. Chill in the refrigerator until firm, 2 to 4 hours. Garnish with the strawberries and whipped cream.

Makes 20 jiggelos

> *"If I forget to tell you later, I had a really good time tonight."*
> —Julia Roberts as Vivian in *Pretty Woman*

Cosmo Royale

Exile

Bloody Good

Swankilicious

Jacks over 7s

The Hem

B-54

Chapter 3

Lounge Lizard

Spin-offs of your Daddy-O's cocktailing, these neotraditionals keep it smoothly cool. Fill your pad with the most groovy, transgenerational party you can and demonstrate your hipness with a few of these jazzy gems and your favorite Rat Pack crooner on CD. Jiggelo is happenin' man!

Cosmo Royale

*If ever a jiggelo were accused of being très chic, it would be the Cosmo Royale.
Part Cosmopolitan and part Kir Royale, this exuberant jiggelo is as pretty as
it is deliciously fun. Women in particular seem to fall for this jiggelo.*

1 (3-ounce) package cranberry-raspberry gelatin or cranberry gelatin
²/₃ cup water
¹/₃ cup Rose's Sweetened Lime Juice
³/₄ cup vodka
¹/₄ cup Triple Sec
1 tablespoon Chambord
Finely grated zest of 1 lime (optional)

Place the gelatin in a heat-resistant bowl. Mix
together the water and Rose's Sweetened Lime
Juice and bring to a boil. Pour the liquid over the
gelatin, stirring until dissolved. Add the vodka,
Triple Sec, and Chambord, mixing well. Divide
the mixture among 20 disposable 1-ounce
cups. Chill in the refrigerator until firm, 2 to
4 hours. Garnish each jiggelo with a pinch
of lime zest.

Makes 20 jiggelos

*"If the drinker has a deep gentleness in him, he
will show that, when drunk. But if he has hidden
anger and arrogance, those appear."*
—Rumi, Sufi poet and whirler

Exile

From Italy, the land of famous exiles—
Napoleon Bonaparte, Pablo Neruda—comes
this inspired jiggelo. An adaptation of the cocktail
Negroni, the symbolic, complex taste of this jiggelo
starts sweet and finishes bitter.

1 (3-ounce) package orange gelatin
1 cup water
$\frac{1}{3}$ cup gin
$\frac{1}{3}$ cup sweet red vermouth
$\frac{1}{3}$ cup Campari
1 (3.5-ounce) can mandarin oranges, drained

Place the gelatin in a heat-resistant bowl. Bring the water to a boil. Pour the water over the gelatin, stirring until dissolved. Add the gin, sweet red vermouth, and Campari, mixing well. Divide the mixture among 20 disposable 1-ounce cups, leaving a little room at the top of each cup. Drop one mandarin orange segment in each jiggelo. Chill in the refrigerator until firm, 2 to 4 hours.

Makes 20 jiggelos

"*Return me, oh Sun, to my wild destiny.*"
—Pablo Neruda, Chilean poet, diplomat,
and exquisitely romantic guy

Bloody Good

Morning, noon, and night, this bloody jiggelo is a delight. There's nothing sweet about it. Instead it has a kick that will add zip to your brunch, burger, or steak. Adding the optional spices makes the taste more satisfyingly complex.

1 cup cold Clamato juice or tomato juice
1 envelope unflavored gelatin
$\frac{1}{2}$ cup citron vodka
$\frac{1}{3}$ cup beer
1 teaspoon Worcestershire sauce
$\frac{1}{2}$ teaspoon lemon extract (do not use lemon juice)
$\frac{1}{4}$ teaspoon wasabi
$\frac{1}{8}$ teaspoon garlic powder
$\frac{1}{8}$ teaspoon ground ginger
Pinch cayenne pepper or more
4 (or more) dashes Tabasco Sauce
$\frac{1}{8}$ teaspoon ground cumin (optional)
$\frac{1}{8}$ teaspoon ground cardamom (optional)
$\frac{1}{8}$ teaspoon ground coriander (optional)
18 small pretzel sticks

Pour the Clamato juice into a small sauce pan and sprinkle with the gelatin. Whisk the mixture well, then let it sit for 3 minutes. Place the pan over medium heat and bring the mixture to a boil, whisking frequently to ensure the gelatin dissolves. Immediately remove the pan from the heat and let the mixture cool for 10 minutes. Add the citron vodka, beer, Worcestershire sauce, lemon extract, wasabi, garlic powder, ginger, cayenne pepper, Tabasco Sauce, cumin, cardamom, and coriander, mixing well. Divide the mixture among 16 to 18 disposable 1-ounce cups. Chill in the refrigerator until firm, 2 to 4 hours. Push a pretzel stick vertically between the jiggelo and each cup before serving. The pretzel can be used to rim the shot.

Makes 16 to 18 jiggelos

"We learned to always keep smiling, even when we're out of Bloody Mary mix."
—Candice Bergen as Sally Weston
in *View from the Top*

Swankilicious

All eyes were on Robert as he swaggered into the room. Women's necks blushed wildly. Certain men's eyebrows raised when they noticed the particular pattern of wear on his pants. Robert understood his power. The power of an icy Pimm's cocktail.

Be a Rob and be one with the Pimm's.

1 (3-ounce) package lemon gelatin
1 cup water
³/₄ cup KeKe Beach
¹/₄ cup Pimm's No. 1

Place the gelatin in a heat-resistant bowl. Bring the water to a boil. Pour the water over the gelatin, stirring until dissolved. Add the KeKe Beach and Pimm's No. 1, mixing well. Divide the mixture among 20 disposable 1-ounce cups. Chill in the refrigerator until firm.

Makes 20 jiggelos

"Zilla keeps rooting for a nice expensive vacation in New York and Atlantic City, with the bright lights and the bootlegged cocktails and a bunch of lounge-lizards to dance with ..."
—Sinclair Lewis, the first American to win
the Nobel Prize for Literature, in *Babbitt*

Jacks over 7s

Two Jacks over 7 and 7—ouch. Don't step up to this table unless you like it real hard and want it badly. Strictly for the gamblers among us. Create them for your next poker night and make yourself some blanks, and you might win for a change.

1 (3-ounce) package lemon gelatin
1 ¼ cup flattened 7-Up (see page 3)
⅓ cup Seagram's 7
⅓ cup Jack Daniels
2 tablespoons Yukon Jack

Place the gelatin in a heat-resistant bowl. Bring the 7-Up to a boil. Pour the 7-Up over the gelatin, stirring until dissolved. Add the Seagram's 7, Jack Daniels, and Yukon Jack, mixing well. Divide the mixture among 20 disposable 1-ounce cups. Chill in the refrigerator until firm, 2 to 4 hours.

Makes 20 jiggelos

"Your mother has this crazy idea that gambling is wrong, even though they say it's OK in the Bible."
—Homer Simpson, couch-potato philosopher and father of America's first family, in *The Simpsons*

The Hem

No twentieth-century American writer romanticized alcohol consumption and edgy living more than Ernest Hemingway. His life spanned four wars, five wives, and countless cocktails. This jiggelo is a version of a cocktail he detailed in Islands in the Stream.

¹/₂ **cup cold water**
¹/₂ **cup Coco López Cream of Coconut**
1 tablespoon Rose's Sweetened Lime Juice
1 envelope unflavored gelatin
¹/₂ **cup gin**
¹/₂ **cup orange rum**
Dash of bitters (optional)

Pour the water, Coco López Cream of Coconut, and Rose's Sweetened Lime Juice in a small sauce pan and sprinkle with the gelatin. Whisk the mixture well, then let it sit for 3 minutes. Place the pan over medium heat and bring the mixture to a boil, whisking frequently to ensure the gelatin dissolves. Immediately remove the pan from the heat and let the mixture cool for 10 minutes. Add the gin, orange rum, and dash of bitters, mixing well. Divide the mixture among 16 to 18 disposable 1-ounce cups. Chill in the refrigerator until firm, 2 to 4 hours.

Makes 16 to 18 jiggelos

> *"Thomas Hudson took a sip of the ice-cold [drink] . . . rewarding to swallow. . . .*
> *It tastes as good as a drawing sail feels, he thought. It is a hell of a good drink."*
> —Ernest Hemingway, a man's man who lived out loud, in *Islands in the Stream*

B-54

We've two-upped the B-52 with this sweet jiggelo. Fifty-four rules! Turn up the "Private Idaho," get out the bingo game, and whip up some B-54s, and you'll have a party any night of the week— these jiggelos are just that good.

½ cup cold toasted almond Coffee-mate
½ cup cold milk
1 envelope unflavored gelatin
⅓ cup Bailey's Irish Cream
⅓ cup Kahlúa
⅓ cup amaretto

Pour the Coffee-mate and milk into a small sauce pan and sprinkle with the gelatin. Whisk the mixture well and let it sit for 3 minutes. Place the pan over medium heat and bring the mixture to a boil, whisking frequently to ensure the gelatin dissolves. Immediately remove the pan from the heat and let the mixture cool for 10 minutes. Add the Bailey's, Kahlúa, and amaretto, mixing well. Divide the mixture among 16 to 18 disposable 1-ounce cups. Chill in the refrigerator until firm, 2 to 4 hours.

Makes 16 to 18 jiggelos.

> *"People get sick, they play the wrong games.*
> *Ya know, it can ruin your name!*
> *Crashers gettin' bombed. (Who's to blame?)"*
> —B-52's, "Party Out of Bounds"

See Scenic America
THE VACATION WONDERLAND

Skid Marks

Twister

Mogul Juice

Horizontal Wonder

Spice, Spice Baby

Hurricane

American Dreamsicle

Chapter 4

American Jiggelo

Perhaps no other beverage is more authentically American than the jiggelo. And like Americans, jiggelos are silly, eclectic, inspired, and often irreverent. Live the jiggelo life!

Skid Marks

Roughly seventeen million spectators attend North American auto races yearly. That's a lot of fried chicken, alcoholic beverages, skid marks, Skol, and mullets. We've alcoholized America's favorite nonalcoholic beer—root beer—to create Skid Marks. Tip: jiggelos are much lighter in the cooler than beer, and they don't spill.

> 1 envelope unflavored gelatin
> 1 cup flattened root beer (see page 3)
> ³/₄ cup root beer schnapps
> ¹/₄ cup vanilla vodka

Pour the root beer into a small sauce pan and sprinkle with the gelatin. Whisk the mixture well, then let it sit for 3 minutes. Place the pan over medium heat and bring the mixture to a boil, whisking frequently to ensure the gelatin dissolves. Immediately remove the pan from the heat and let the mixture cool for 10 minutes. Add the root beer schnapps and vanilla vodka, mixing well. Divide the mixture among 16 to 18 disposable 1-ounce cups. Chill in the refrigerator until firm, 2 to 4 hours.

Makes 16 to 18 jiggelos

"If you're trying at all to live up to the race-driver image [during May in Indy], you've been drunk twenty times, laid thirty-five, had twenty hangovers, and blown two engines. . . . Damn, racing is fun."
—A. J. Foyt, *A. J.: My Life as America's Greatest Race Car Driver*

Twister

There's a whole lot of twisting going on. In 1966, the year the game Twister was introduced, there were 585 tornados. Twister, the juice line, hit the shelves in 1988, and in the same year 702 tornados hit the U.S. In 1996, when the Twister *movie appeared, 1,173 tornados occurred. Now twist your tongue around these entwined flavors.*

1 (3-ounce) package strawberry kiwi gelatin or strawberry gelatin
1 cup water
¹/₂ cup vodka
¹/₄ cup peach schnapps
¹/₄ cup Midori

Place the gelatin in a heat-resistant bowl. Bring the water to a boil. Pour the water over the gelatin, stirring until dissolved. Add the vodka, peach schnapps, and Midori, mixing well. Divide the mixture among 20 disposable 1-ounce cups. Chill in the refrigerator until firm, 2 to 4 hours.

Makes 20 jiggelos

"Shy Shelly says she shall sew sheets."
—Tongue twister

Mogul Juice

Survival or enjoyment? That's what many of the fifty-seven million U.S. skiers asked themselves last year. It's all about absorbing those violent undulations of your knees and skis. And après ski, it's about absorbing this spiced cider–inspired jiggelo and enjoying friends around a crackling fire.

> 1 cup cold apple cider
> 1 envelope unflavored gelatin
> ⅓ cup buttershots
> ⅓ cup apple schnapps
> ⅓ cup spiced rum
> ⅛ teaspoon ground cinnamon (optional)
> Pinch of ground nutmeg (optional)

Pour the cider into a small sauce pan and sprinkle with the gelatin. Whisk the mixture well, then let it sit for 3 minutes. Place the pan over medium heat and bring the mixture to a boil, whisking frequently to ensure the gelatin dissolves. Immediately remove the pan from the heat and let the mixture cool for 10 minutes. Add the buttershots, apple schnapps, spiced rum, cinnamon, and nutmeg, mixing well. Divide the mixture among 16 to 18 disposable 1-ounce cups. Chill in the refrigerator until firm, 2 to 4 hours.

Makes 16 to 18 jiggelos

"Skiing combines outdoor fun with knocking down trees with your face."
—Dave Barry, Famous Floridian and Pulitzer Prize–winning humorist

Horizontal Wonder

Have you ever driven across the middle of Kansas? And driven. And driven. Then you know what we're talking about. You could start a cranberry rolling in Limon, Colorado, and it wouldn't stop until it hit Kansas City! Rejoice in the staggering, minimalist beauty of the Plains States with this jiggelo that's particularly wonderful with barbecue.

1 (3-ounce) package cranberry gelatin
⅔ cup water
⅓ cup orange juice
½ cup orange rum
½ cup crema di limoni, or ⅓ cup lemoncello and 2 tablespoons cream

Place the gelatin in a heat-resistant bowl. Mix together the water and orange juice and bring to a boil. Pour the liquid over the gelatin, stirring until dissolved. Add the orange rum and crema di limoni and mix well. Divide the mixture among 20 disposable 1-ounce cups. Chill in the refrigerator until firm, 2 to 4 hours.

Makes 20 jiggelos

> *"When I write, I aim in my mind not toward New York but toward a vague spot a little to the east of Kansas."*
> —John Updike, prolific American writer with yummy brown eyes

Spice, Spice Baby

Coca-Cola was invented in 1886 by an Atlanta pharmacist looking for a headache cure. Now every 60 seconds 756,000 people the world over reach for a Coca-Cola, the genuine, quintessential American beverage. Add new meaning to your cola with this spicy jiggelo.

1 (3-ounce) package black cherry gelatin
1¼ cup flattened cola soda (see page 3)
⅔ cup spiced rum
1 tablespoon grenadine

Place the gelatin in a heat-resistant bowl. Bring the cola to a boil. Pour the cola over the gelatin, stirring until dissolved. Add the spiced rum and grenadine, mixing well. Divide the mixture among 20 disposable 1-ounce cups. Chill in the refrigerator until firm, 2 to 4 hours.

Makes 20 jiggelos

"When I think of Indonesia—a country on the equator with 180 million people, a median age of 18, and a Muslim ban on alcohol—I feel I know what heaven looks like."
—Anonymous cola-company official

Hurricane

*Hurricanes not only have many names—
David, Camille, Isabel—they have named
many things, including several liqueur-
based beverages, theme park rides, a kind
of tall cocktail glass, lots of coastal
restaurants, and now a jiggelo!*

1 (3-ounce) package raspberry gelatin
1 cup water
⅓ cup gin
⅓ cup citron vodka
⅓ cup blue curaçao

Place the gelatin in a heat-resistant bowl.
Bring the water to a boil. Pour the water over
the gelatin, stirring until dissolved. Add the
gin, citron vodka, and blue curaçao, mixing
well. Divide the mixture among 20 disposable
1-ounce cups. Chill in the refrigerator until
firm, 2 to 4 hours.

Makes 20 jiggelos

*"I'll always be the Hurricane,
and a hurricane is beautiful."*
—Denzel Washington as Rubin
"Hurricane" Carter in
The Hurricane

*"Ice cream is exquisite.
What a pity it isn't illegal."*
—Voltaire, French philosopher who
relentlessly questioned authority

American Dreamsicle

Remember pausing from the slip 'n slide to chase the ice cream man? Can't you just feel your bare feet on the hot pavement as your tongue seeks the cold dreaminess of a creamsicle? Make batches of these childhood-inspired jiggelos, turn on the sprinkler, and invite the neighborhood over!

1 (3-ounce) package orange gelatin
²/₃ cup water
¹/₃ cup orange juice
¹/₂ cup vanilla vodka
¹/₄ cup raspberry vodka or other berry vodka
¹/₄ cup KeKe Beach

Place the gelatin in a heat-resistant bowl. Mix together the water and orange juice and bring to a boil. Pour the liquid over the gelatin, stirring until dissolved. Add the vanilla vodka, raspberry vodka, and KeKe Beach, mixing well. Divide the mixture among 20 disposable 1-ounce cups. Chill in the refrigerator until firm, 2 to 4 hours.

Makes 20 jiggelos

Cheeky Tiki
Panda Antics
Vs.
Orangerie
Insomniac City
Martinique Mojo
Cradle

Chapter 5

Global Swarming

Fusion imbibing at its best. Jiggelos embrace the world view and works some international mix-master magic. Think theme gatherings and enjoy the multicultural madness. *Á vôtre santé!*

Cheeky Tiki

Long before Pan-Asian trendiness was conceived, Tiki was chic. Born in the '40s and newly rediscovered, the Tiki movement is an exuberant state of island-being. You'll find this rum-a-luscious tropical jiggelo is right at home next to the pu pu platter.

1 (3-ounce) package pineapple gelatin
1 cup water
½ cup coconut rum
¼ cup orange rum
¼ cup banana rum

Place the gelatin in a heat-resistant bowl. Bring the water to a boil. Pour the water over the gelatin, stirring until dissolved. Add the coconut rum, orange rum, and banana rum, mixing well. Divide the mixture among 20 disposable 1-ounce cups. Chill in the refrigerator until firm, 2 to 4 hours.

Makes 20 jiggelos

"Mekkalekka hi, Mekkahiney ho."
—Pee-Wee and Tito in *Pee-Wee's Playhouse*

Panda Antics

The world seems panda crazy—except perhaps pandas. They can't even manage interest in copulation! We propose researchers make these subtle jiggelos and play some Barry White. Try this clearly unusual and surprising shot yourself and enjoy the antics! If you don't have AriZona tea, you can brew your own green tea or peppermint tea, sweeten it with honey, and chill it.

1 cup chilled AriZona Green Tea with Ginseng and Honey
1 envelope unflavored gelatin
1 cup sake
16 to 18 red gummy bears

Pour tea into a small sauce pan and sprinkle with the gelatin. Whisk the mixture well, then let it sit for 3 minutes. Place the pan over medium heat and bring the mixture to a boil, whisking frequently. Immediately remove the pan from the heat and let the mixture cool for 10 minutes. Add the sake, mixing well. Divide the mixture among 16 to 18 disposable 1-ounce cups, leaving $1/2$ inch of space at the top of each cup. Chill for 40 minutes and then push a gummy bear into each shot, using a toothpick to position the bear. Chill in the refrigerator until firm, 2 to 4 hours.

Makes 16 to 18 jiggelos

"Ghengdu, China—China is flicking on sex videos . . . to rouse the dreary desires of captive male giant pandas. . . . Didi . . . sat eyes glued in front of a screen that showed a video of two giant pandas mating. . . . 'Didi seemed to like his gift immensely.'"
—www.cnn.com

Vs.

As the Russia-vs.-U.S. rivalry collapses, we now understand that we're a lot more alike than we are different:

	Russia	**USA**
Population:	144,526,278	290,342,554
Median age:	37.6 years	35.8 years
Population growth rate:	-0.3%	0.92%
Sex ratio at birth:	1.05 males/females	1.05 males/females
Literacy:	99.6%	97%
Electricity consumption:	773.08 billion kWh	3.479 trillion kWh
Cellular telephones:	19 million	69.209 million
External debt:	$153.5 billion	$862 billion
HIV/AIDS adult prevalence rate:	0.9%	0.06%
Total area:	17,075,200 sq. miles	9,629,091 sq. miles
Gross Domestic Product per capita:	$9,300	$37,600
Population below the poverty line:	25%	12.7%

—source: www.cia.gov

Embrace camaraderie with these comfortable, vodkafied jiggelos.

1 (3-ounce) package grape gelatin
1 cup boiling water
$\frac{1}{2}$ cup orange vodka
$\frac{1}{4}$ cup citron vodka
$\frac{1}{4}$ cup Southern Comfort

Place the gelatin in a heat-resistant bowl. Bring the water to a boil. Pour the water over the gelatin, stirring until dissolved. Add the orange vodka, citron vodka, and Southern Comfort, mixing well. Divide the mixture among 20 disposable 1-ounce cups. Chill in the refrigerator until firm, 2 to 4 hours.

Makes 20 jiggelos

"I took a speed reading course and read War and Peace in twenty minutes. It involves Russia."
—Woody Allen, neurotic New York writer on the edge of eye-wear fashion trends

Orangerie

Before it was home to Claude Monet's astonishing, panoramic water lily paintings, Paris's Musée de l'Orangerie was a hothouse that kept the royalty's potted orange trees from freezing. Conversely, before your refrigerator was home to these twenty precious and very orangey jiggelos, it was a cold-house that kept your condiments healthy.

1 (3-ounce) package orange gelatin
1 cup water
¹/₂ cup orange vodka
¹/₄ cup blue curaçao
¹/₄ cup Cointreau
1 (3.5-ounce) can mandarin oranges (optional)

Place the gelatin in a heat-resistant bowl. Bring the water to a boil. Pour the water over the gelatin, stirring until dissolved. Add the orange vodka, blue curaçao, and Cointreau, mixing well. Divide among 20 disposable 1-ounce cups leaving a little room in each cup. Place one mandarin orange segment in each cup. Chill in the refrigerator until firm, 2 to 4 hours.

Makes 20 jiggelos

"As an artist, a man has no home in Europe save in Paris."
—Friedrich Nietzsche, German existentialist philosopher who advocated
life-affirming questioning before Dr. Phil was born

Insomniac City

This shot is dedicated to NYC, the city that never sleeps. Why would anyone choose to sleep in the world's most stimulating city? And such a fine insomniac jiggelo this is! Not too sweet but very coffee-yummy.

²/₃ **cup cold milk**
¹/₃ **cup room-temperature coffee**
1 envelope unflavored gelatin
¹/₂ **cup Kahlúa**
¹/₃ **cup vodka**
¹/₄ **cup Frangelico**

Pour the milk and coffee into a small sauce pan and sprinkle with the gelatin. Whisk the mixture well, then let it sit for 3 minutes. Place the pan over medium heat and bring the mixture to a boil, whisking frequently to ensure the gelatin dissolves. Immediately remove the pan from the heat and let the mixture cool for 10 minutes. Add the Kahlúa, vodka, and Frangelico, mixing well. Divide the mixture among 16 to 18 disposable 1-ounce cups. Chill in the refrigerator until firm, 2 to 4 hours.

Makes 16 to 18 jiggelos

"Life is something that happens when you can't get to sleep."
—Fran Lebowitz, sardonic New York writer and renowned smoker

Martinique Mojo

Inspired by the magical lushness of a French Caribbean island, this jiggelo employs Martinique's native staple of bananas. For a pseudoromantic experience, slather yourself with coconut-scented suntan lotion and add an exotically accented cabana boy to the party.

1 (3-ounce) package strawberry-banana gelatin
1 cup water
¼ cup orange rum
¼ cup pineapple rum
¼ cup dark rum
¼ cup crème de banane
1 (3.5-ounce) can mandarin oranges (optional)
1 tablespoon shredded coconut (optional)

Place the gelatin in a heat-resistant bowl. Bring the water to a boil. Pour the water over the gelatin, stirring until dissolved. Add the orange rum, pineapple rum, dark rum, and crème de banane, mixing well. Divide among 20 disposable 1-ounce cups leaving a little room in each. Place one mandarin orange segment in each cup. Chill in the refrigerator until firm, 2 to 4 hours. Place a pinch of shredded coconut on top of each jiggelo prior to serving.

Makes 20 jiggelos

"The most delicious thing in the world is a banana."
—Benjamin Disraeli, British Prime Minister, dandy, and epicurean

Cradle

Africa is known as the Cradle of Civilization. Egypt has a five-thousand-year-old mummy. Chad has a six- or seven-million-year-old human fossil. And humans first began mastering the challenge of cultivation in Africa. Challenge your concept of gelatin shots with this highly unusual and spicy Afrinspired jiggelo. This jiggelo separates while chilling to create a creamy peanut butter topping!

> 1 (3-ounce) package pineapple gelatin
> 2 tablespoon creamy peanut butter (not the all-natural variety)
> 1 cup water
> ²/₃ cup pineapple rum
> ¹/₃ cup vodka
> 4 (or more) dashes Tabasco Sauce

Place the gelatin and peanut butter in a heat-resistant bowl. Bring the water to a boil. Pour the water over the gelatin, whisking until the gelatin is dissolved and the peanut butter is evenly distributed. Add the pineapple rum, vodka, and Tabasco Sauce, mixing well. Divide the mixture among 20 to 22 disposable 1-ounce cups. Chill in the refrigerator until firm, 2 to 4 hours.

Makes 20 to 22 jiggelos

"A camel does not tease another camel about his humps."
—Egyptian proverb

Paternity Sample
Aurora Borealis
Rapture
Synchronicity
Tree Hugger
Smoothie
Drunken Donuts
Summit

Chapter 6

Quantum Whatever

Alchemy is the heart of jiggelo. Wherever there is alchemy, there is astro-thermal-symbiotics. Wherever there is astro-thermal-symbiotics, a quandary is near. And wherever there is a quandary, "whatever" is just around the corner. These jiggelos may have greater difficulty levels, but we bet your scores will be high!

Paternity Sample

Who knew that paternity would spawn an industry? Thanks to Maury, Jenny, Jerry, and the wonders of DNA testing, dysfunctional and disturbing intimacies have become spectacles. Girls, if you're gonna play with jiggelos, make sure to do so safely!

3 graham cracker squares, crushed
1 (3-ounce) package mixed fruit gelatin
1 cup water
½ cup banana rum
¼ cup tequila
¼ cup crème de cassis
1 (3.5-ounce) snack-size container of vanilla pudding

Sprinkle the graham cracker crumbs in the bottom of 22 disposable 1-ounce cups.

Place the gelatin in a heat-resistant bowl. Bring the water to a boil. Pour the water over the gelatin, stirring until dissolved. Add the banana rum, tequila, and crème de cassis, mixing well. Divide the mixture among the cups, leaving ½ inch of space at the top of each cup. Chill for 30 minutes and then drop a teaspoon of vanilla pudding into each cup.
Chill in the refrigerator until firm, 1½ to 2½ hours.

Makes 22 jiggelos

"We are going to play a fun game. It's called, 'who is your daddy and what does he do?'"
—Arnold Schwartzenegger as Detective John Kimble
in *Kindergarten Cop*

Aurora Borealis

The aurora borealis occurs in the Northern Hemisphere when gaseous matter thrown off by the sun hits the earth's atmosphere. The resulting nocturnal performance is like the sheerest luminescent scarf being twirled through the night sky by invisible dancing angels. Perhaps this two-layered jiggelo isn't quite as poetic, but its alluring translucency and flecks of gold are entertaining.

Bottom Layer

- 1 cup cold water
- 1 envelope unflavored gelatin
- 1 cup apple schnapps
- $\frac{1}{3}$ cup Goldschläger
- 3 drops blue food coloring
- 3 drops red food coloring

Pour the cold water into a small sauce pan and sprinkle with the gelatin. Whisk the mixture well, then let it sit for 3 minutes. Place the pan over medium heat and bring the mixture to a boil, whisking frequently to ensure the gelatin dissolves. Immediately remove the pan from the heat and let the mixture cool for 10 minutes. Add the apple schnapps, Goldschläger, and food coloring, mixing well. Fill 40 disposable 1-ounce cups half full. Chill in the refrigerator 1 hour and then begin making the top layer.

Top Layer

- 1 cup cold water
- 1 envelope unflavored gelatin
- $\frac{3}{4}$ cup vanilla vodka
- $\frac{1}{4}$ cup vanilla schnapps
- 4 drops blue food coloring

Follow the directions for the first layer to the point when the pan is removed from the heat. Add vanilla vodka, vanilla schnapps, and blue food coloring, mixing well. Refrigerate this mixture for 15 minutes and then pour on top of the bottom layer. Chill in the refrigerator until firm, 2 to 3 hours.

Makes 40 cosmic jiggelos

"I'd like to know / What this whole show / Is all about / Before it's out."
—Piet Hein, scientist, poet, and the world's most quoted Scandinavian

Rapture

Call it what you will—a candy bar disguised as a jiggelo or a jiggelo disguised as a candy bar. Whatever. It's certainly the catalyst for rapture! Everything good in one delicious slurp—butterscotch, cookies, chocolate, nuts. Love should be so dependably sweet.

"No pleasure, no rapture, no exquisite sin greater . . . than central air."
—Jason Lee as Azrael in *Dogma*

12 vanilla wafers, crushed
1 cup cold milk
1 envelope unflavored gelatin
⅓ cup buttershots
⅓ cup Frangelico
2 tablespoons butterscotch topping
1 (3.5-ounce) snack-size container butterscotch pudding
2 to 3 teaspoons chocolate Magic Shell
1 tablespoon chopped nuts (optional)
1 tablespoon grated chocolate (optional)

Sprinkle the crushed vanilla wafers in the bottom of 20 disposable 1-ounce cups.

Pour the milk into a small sauce pan and sprinkle with the gelatin. Whisk well, then let sit for 3 minutes. Place the pan over medium heat and bring the mixture to a boil, whisking well to ensure the gelatin dissolves. Immediately remove the pan from the heat and let the mixture cool for 10 minutes. Add the buttershots, Frangelico, butterscotch topping, and butterscotch pudding, mixing well. Fill the cups half full and chill in the refrigerator for 1 hour. Half of the mixture should be remaining. Cover it and let it sit at room temperature.

After the jiggelos have chilled for 1 hour, remove them from the refrigerator. Carefully squeeze a nickel-sized drop of Magic Shell in the center of each jiggelo. (The Magic Shell should not extend to the edges of the container, or you will have difficulty slurping it without rimming.) Place jiggelos in the freezer for 5 minutes or refrigerator for 15 minutes, or until the Magic Shell hardens.

Whisk the remaining gelatin mixture well and distribute it among the cups. Chill in the refrigerator until firm, 1 to 2 hours.

Prior to serving, sprinkle each jiggelo with a few nuts and grated chocolate.

Makes 20 jiggelos

Synchronicity

It's a peculiar feeling when the unrelated suddenly take on characteristics of being meaningfully related. We think of it as the Universe confirming that you are on the right path. And we're pretty sure the Universe wants you to make these three-layered symbiotic jiggelos to share with serendipitous friends. The middle layer is a tiny shot of tequila.

"A star fall, a phone call,
It joins all, Synchronicity"
—Sting, *Synchronicity*

Bottom Layer
> **1 (3-ounce) package raspberry gelatin**
> **1½ cups water**
> **½ cup berry vodka**

Place the gelatin in a heat-resistant bowl. Bring the water to a boil. Pour the water over the gelatin, stirring until dissolved. Add the berry vodka, mixing well. Fill 40 disposable 1-ounce cups half full. Chill in the refrigerator for 1 hour and then proceed with the next layer.

Top Layer
> **1 (3-ounce) package lemon gelatin**
> **1½ cups water**
> **½ cup citron vodka**

Follow the directions for the first layer substituting lemon gelatin for raspberry gelatin and citron vodka for the berry vodka. Let the mixture chill in the refrigerator for 30 minutes.

Middle Layer and Final Assembly
> **1 cup tequila**

Remove half-full jiggelos and the top-layer mixture from the refrigerator. Pour 1 teaspoon tequila over the bottom layer in each cup. Slowly fill the cups with the top-layer mixture. Chill in the refrigerator for 2 hours.

Makes 40 jiggelos

Tree Hugger Smoothie

Make this delicious natural jiggelo for your vegetarian or vegan friends or make it for all those you care about because it's good for them. It tastes awesome, too. Gathering the ingredients is the biggest challenge, but all the love that comes back to you will be worth it. Please read the tips on using Hain SuperFruits Dessert Mix (page 3).

- $1/2$ **cup carrot juice**
- $1/2$ **cup soy milk**
- **1 tablespoon honey**
- **1 (3-ounce) package orange Hain SuperFruits Dessert Mix (see Resources, page 88)**
- $1/4$ **cup vodka**
- **2 tablespoons Cointreau**
- **2 teaspoons finely chopped fresh mint (optional)**
- **2 tablespoons granola (optional)**

Mix together the carrot juice, soy milk, and honey, and bring the mixture to a boil. Place the Hain SuperFruits Dessert Mix in a heat-resistant bowl and pour the liquid over the powder, stirring until dissolved. Add the vodka, Cointreau, and mint, mixing well. Divide the mixture among 20 disposable 1-ounce cups. Chill in the refrigerator until firm, 2 to 4 hours. Garnish with a light sprinkle of granola prior to serving.

Makes 20 jiggelos

Kelly: "They make you, like, feed a tree before you feed yourself."
Ozzy: "How the fuck you feed a tree? What—you put a ham sandwich on the tree?"
—Kelly and Ozzy Osbourne, *The Osbournes*

Drunken Donuts

Mexico has a way with coffee that makes it worth waking for. With Mexican syrup and donut holes, you have a jiggelo worthy of any time of day. There are two steps in the creation of this jiggelo. The first is making the Mexican syrup, a spicy ambrosia that can be stored in the refrigerator for up to 5 days. (You'll have enough for the jiggelo recipe and plenty extra to use in the weekend's coffee.) The second step is assembling the jiggelos. Make sure you select a brand of donut hole that will fit the size of cup you are using.

"Coffee without caffeine is like sex without the spanking."
—Jeremy Piven as Trevor Hale in *Cupid*

Mexican Syrup

1 1/2 cup water
1/3 cup packed brown sugar
Peel from an orange, roughly chopped
2 cinnamon sticks, broken into pieces

Place the water, brown sugar, orange peel, and cinnamon sticks into a small sauce pan and bring the mixture to a boil over medium heat. When boiling begins, reduce the heat so that the mixture just simmers. Allow the mixture to simmer for 15 minutes, or until the liquid is reduced by half. Cool the mixture and strain it. Place the liquid in an airtight container and store in the refrigerator until ready for use. The syrup can be stored in the refrigerator for up to 5 days.

Jiggelos

2/3 cup Mexican Syrup
2/3 cup chilled coffee
1 envelope unflavored gelatin
1/2 cup vanilla rum
4 tablespoons tequila
18 to 20 donut holes

Place the Mexican Syrup and coffee in a small sauce pan and sprinkle with gelatin. Whisk the mixture well and let it sit for 3 minutes. Place the pan over medium heat and bring to a boil, whisking frequently to ensure the gelatin dissolves. Immediately remove the pan from the heat and let the mixture cool for 10 minutes. Add the vanilla rum and tequila, mixing well. Divide the mixture among 20 disposable 1-ounce cups, leaving 1/2 inch of space at the top of each cup. Chill in the refrigerator 40 minutes. Place one donut hole in each jiggelo, pressing the donut hole down so that half is submerged and half is above the gelatin. Chill in the refrigerator until firm, for 1 to 2 hours.

Makes 20 jiggelos and extra Mexican Syrup

Summit

Here it is—the pinnacle of jiggelosity! A three-layered shot inspired by the multi-layered ice cream delicacy, Neapolitan. Yeah, it's a little time consuming. But when you're finished, you'll have fifty-four of the most handsome, intoxicatingly delectable jiggelos known to humans. You can always make just one third of each layer for a yield of eighteen jiggelos, but you'll be sorry. People can't keep their hands off this jiggelo!

"Truth is the summit of being . . ."
—Ralph Waldo Emerson, American
transcendentalist philosopher
and writer

Bottom Layer

1 cup cold chocolate milk
1 envelope unflavored gelatin
²/₃ cup Godiva liqueur
¹/₃ cup crème de cacao

Pour the chocolate milk into a small sauce pan and sprinkle with gelatin. Whisk the mixture well, then let sit for 3 minutes. Place the pan over medium heat and bring the mixture to a boil, whisking frequently to ensure the gelatin dissolves. Immediately remove the pan from the heat and let the mixture cool for 10 minutes. Add the Godiva liqueur and crème de cacao, mixing well. Fill 54 disposable 1-ounce cups one-third full. Chill in the refrigerator at least 1 hour before beginning to make the following middle layer.

Middle Layer

1 cup cold milk
1 teaspoon vanilla extract
1 envelope unflavored gelatin
¹/₂ cup vanilla vodka
¹/₂ cup vanilla schnapps

Follow directions the for bottom layer, substituting milk and vanilla extract for the chocolate milk, and substituting vanilla vodka and vanilla schnapps for the Godiva liqueur and crème de cacao. Pour the mixture over the bottom layer in each cup, filling the cup only two-thirds full. Chill in the refrigerator at least 1 hour before beginning to make the following top layer.

Top Layer

1 cup cold strawberry milk
1 envelope unflavored gelatin
**1/2 cup crème de strawberry or
     strawberry schnapps**
1/2 cup Tequila Rose

Follow the directions for the bottom layer, substituting strawberry milk for the chocolate milk, and substituting crème de strawberry and Tequila Rose for the Godiva liqueur and crème de cacao. Pour the mixture over the middle layer, filling the cup. Chill in the refrigerator until firm, 2 to 3 hours.

Makes 54 jiggelos

Cult of Minthe
Twinkle Dare
Brûlette
Baby Boba
Cordial Rose
Crazy Ho
Miraculous Conception
Ginger-Citrus Party Poke Cake
Chocolate-Raspberry Party Poke Cake

Chapter 7

Our Must Desserts

What could be more perfect than a dessert that makes you smile inside and out? A dessert that meets every fathomable dessert desire. A smooth and chewy solid liquid that's lightly rich and sensorially intoxicating—dessert jiggelos. Indulge!

Cult of Minthe

This jiggelo is dedicated to Minthe, the Greek nymph who was changed into an herb by Hades's jealous wife, Persephone. Perchance Persephone's resentful mood might have improved with a little chocolate? You'll join the Cult of Minthe, too, after one tiny taste of this rich choco-mint sinfulness.

1 cup cold chocolate milk
1 envelope unflavored gelatin
²⁄₃ cup crème de menthe
¹⁄₃ cup crème de cacao
48 to 54 chocolate chips (optional)
16 to 18 fresh mint leaves (optional)

Pour the chocolate milk into a small sauce pan and sprinkle with the gelatin. Whisk the mixture well, then let it sit for 3 minutes. Place the pan over medium heat and bring the mixture to a boil, whisking frequently. Immediately remove the pan from the heat and let the mixture cool for 10 minutes. Add the crème de menthe and the crème de cacao, mixing well. Place three chocolate chips in 16 to 18 disposable 1-ounce cups. Divide the mixture among the cups. Chill in the refrigerator until firm, 2 to 4 hours. Garnish each jiggelo with a fresh mint leaf.

Makes 16 to 18 jiggelos

"I am that flower—That mint. That columbine."
—William Shakespeare, playwright and prodigious
   word inventor, in *Love's Labor's Lost*

Twinkle Dare

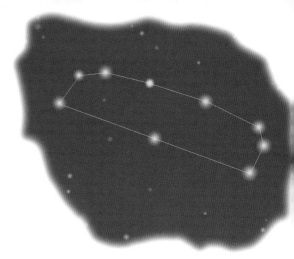

Twinkle, twinkle, Twinkie cake,
with you a jiggelo dessert I make.
So quick, so easy, so light as air,
what could be more fun than Twinkle Dare?

1 (3-ounce) package strawberry gelatin
1 cup water
$\frac{1}{2}$ cup crème de strawberry
$\frac{1}{4}$ cup brandy
$\frac{1}{4}$ cup peach schnapps
2 Twinkies
Cooking spray
1 (7-ounce) can whipped cream (optional)
8 to 12 fresh strawberries (optional)

Place the gelatin in a heat-resistant bowl. Bring the water to a boil. Pour water over the gelatin, stirring until dissolved. Add the crème de strawberry, brandy, and peach schnapps, stirring well. Lightly spray a rectangular 3-cup plastic container with cooking spray. Pour the mixture into the container. Unwrap the Twinkies and submerge them with the bottom side up. Keep gentle pressure on the Twinkies until they absorb enough gelatin so that the bottoms of the Twinkies are flush with the top of the gelatin. Chill in the refrigerator until firm, 4 to 5 hours. Invert the gelatin onto a plate. Cut the Twinkle Dare into slices with a knife that has been warmed in hot water. Serve on plates and garnish with whipped cream and fresh strawberries.

Serves 4 to 6

"Real programmers don't eat quiche. They eat Twinkies and Szechuan food."
—Unknown

Brûlette

Never was there a more ou-la-la dessert than crème brûlèe. Astound your guests with these tiny Brûlettes, complete with classic dark sugar, and they'll be shouting, "Encore!" Bow deeply and serve more with a smile. No one has to know how easy it was.

1 cup cold milk
1 envelope unflavored gelatin
1/2 cup vanilla schnapps
1/4 cup vanilla vodka
1/4 cup Frangelico
2 tablespoons instant vanilla pudding mix
4 to 4 1/2 teaspoons of packed brown sugar

Pour the milk into a small sauce pan and sprinkle with the gelatin. Whisk the mixture well, then let it sit for 3 minutes. Place the pan over medium heat and bring the mixture to a boil, whisking frequently to ensure the gelatin dissolves. Immediately remove the pan from the heat and let the mixture cool for 10 minutes. Add the vanilla schnapps, vanilla vodka, Frangelico, and instant vanilla pudding mix. Put 1/4 teaspoon of packed brown sugar in each of 16 to 18 disposable 1-ounce cups. Divide the mixture among the cups. Chill in the refrigerator until firm, 2 to 4 hours.

Makes 16 to 18 jiggelos

"We write to taste life twice, in the moment and in retrospection."
—Anaïs Nin, French-American writer and chronic diarist, in *The Diary of Anaïs Nin*

Baby Boba

As technology shrinks the planet, the half-life of trends grows ever shorter. Boba, a drink with marble-sized tapioca bouncing around in it, is a beverage fad that began in Taiwan in the '90s. Quickly usurped by fashion-conscious beverage boutiques, bobas are popping up everywhere. Hop on this n-o-w trend before it's gone and make a Baby Boba—an inventive, delectable jiggelo with tapioca pudding suspended in it.

1 (3-ounce) package apricot gelatin or peach gelatin
1 cup water
½ cup vodka
¼ cup peach schnapps
2 tablespoons Chambord
1 (3.5-ounce) snack-size container of tapioca pudding

Place the gelatin in a heat-resistant bowl. Bring the water to a boil. Pour the water over the gelatin, stirring until dissolved. Add the vodka, peach schnapps, Chambord, and tapioca pudding, mixing well. Divide the mixture among 22 to 24 disposable 1-ounce cups, or alternatively, pour into two prepared ice cube trays (see page 4). Chill in the refrigerator until firm, 2 to 4 hours. If using ice cube trays, unmold and serve on plates.

Makes 22 to 24 jiggelos

"Fashion is a form of ugliness so intolerable that we have to alter it every six months."
—Oscar Wilde, English author, playwright, and bisexual rascal

Cordial Rose

Got Tequila Rose? We want to personally thank the genius who invented this creamy strawberry-tequila liqueur! Dang, Eunice, what a joy! Using tiny chocolate cordial cups as your edible container for this jiggelo creates a virtually immoral pleasure. Warning! Chocolate cordial cups hold only one third ounce, so you will find them quickly and happily consumed.

"It was my Uncle George who discovered that alcohol was a food well in advance of modern medical thought."
—P. G. Wodehouse, English satirist, in *The Inimitable Jeeves*

1 cup cold milk
1 envelope unflavored gelatin
1 (1.25-ounce) package instant hot cocoa mix
$\frac{1}{2}$ cup Tequila Rose
$\frac{1}{3}$ cup Godiva liqueur
1 tablespoons Cointreau
52 to 56 chocolate cordial cups, chilled (see Resources page 88),
    or 48 to 56 chocolate chips
1 (7-ounce) can whipped cream (optional)

Pour the milk into a small sauce pan and sprinkle with the gelatin. Whisk the mixture well, then let it sit for 3 minutes. Place the pan over medium heat and bring the mixture to a boil, whisking frequently to ensure the gelatin dissolves. Immediately remove the pan from the heat and let the mixture cool for 10 minutes. Add the Tequila Rose, Godiva liqueur, and Cointreau, mixing well. Chill the mixture in the refrigerator for 20 minutes. Divide the mixture among the chocolate cups and chill in the refrigerator until firm, 1 to 2 hours. If not using chocolate cordial cups, place 3 chocolate chips in the bottom of 16 to 18 disposable 1-ounce cups. Divide the mixture among the cups and chill in the refrigerator until firm, 2 to 4 hours. Garnish with whipped cream.

Makes 52 to 56 tiny jiggelos or 16 to 18 regular jiggelos

Crazy Ho

In 1967, about the same time serious experimentation with gelatin shots was occurring, the HoHo was invented in San Francisco. Today Hostess bakes a mile of snack cakes every 22 minutes, and they should be put to the best use possible. Don't be daunted, this is a simple recipe that is both amazingly delicious and crazy fun. For a larger party, use a standard size loaf pan and double the recipe.

¹/₄ **cup cold water**
¹/₄ **cup room-temperature coffee**
1 envelope unflavored gelatin
¹/₄ **cup Godiva liqueur**
¹/₄ **cup chocolate vodka**
2 tablespoons Cointreau
3 HoHos, 2 unwrapped
Cooking spray
1 (7-ounce) can whipped cream (optional)

In a small sauce pan mix together the water and coffee and sprinkle with the gelatin. Whisk the mixture well and let it sit for 3 minutes. Place the pan over medium heat and bring the mixture to a boil, stirring frequently. Immediately remove the pan from the heat and let the mixture cool for 10 minutes. Add the Godiva liqueur, chocolate vodka, and Cointreau, mixing well. Lightly spray a rectangular 3-cup container with cooking spray. Pour the mixture into the container. Place the two unwrapped HoHos in the mixture, bottom sides up. They will float. Let them rest for 2 minutes and then place third, still wrapped, HoHo on top. (This will provide just enough weight to hold the other HoHos under the gelatin.) Chill the mixture in the refrigerator for 40 minutes, then remove the unwrapped HoHo and reserve for another use. Continue chilling the mixture until firm, another 2 hours. (Chilling over 3 to 4 hours will make the HoHos' chocolate coating difficult to slice through neatly.)

Invert the gelatin onto a plate. Cut the Crazy Ho into slices with a knife that has been warmed in hot water. Cut the gelatin in the direction that shows the pin wheels and serve on plates. Garnish with whipped cream.

Serves 4 to 6

Miraculous Conception

When the peanut butter fell into the jiggelo, we let it be. Three hours later, we were stunned to discover that the peanut butter separated while chilling, creating delightful and perfect layers. Naturally, we had to pair it with chocolate. The results are as delectable as they are dramatic.

$^{1}/_{2}$ **cup cold water**
$^{1}/_{2}$ **cup cold milk**
1 envelope unflavored gelatin
2 tablespoons smooth peanut butter (not the all-natural variety)
$^{1}/_{2}$ **cup chocolate vodka**
$^{1}/_{4}$ **cup amaretto**
1 tablespoon chocolate syrup

Place the water and milk in a small sauce pan and sprinkle with the gelatin. Whisk the mixture well, then let it sit for 3 minutes. Place the pan over medium heat and bring to boil, stirring frequently to ensure the gelatin dissolves. Immediately remove the pan from the heat and add the peanut butter, incorporating it well. Let the mixture cool for 10 minutes. Add the chocolate vodka, amaretto, and chocolate sauce, mixing well. Divide among 16 to 18 disposable 1-ounce cups. Chill in the refrigerator until firm, 2 to 4 hours.

Makes 16 to 18 jiggelos

"Only those who will risk going too far can possibly find out how far one can go."
—T. S. Eliot, handsome Amer-British poet and critic

Ginger-Citrus Party Poke Cake

Our grandmothers used to make a nonalcoholic version of this cake, so a playful adaptation was only natural. Jiggelo, the contemporary gelatin shot, wed to classic, comfort food gingerbread. Mmmm. Seconds, please!

Bonus: You'll get a few jiggelos on the side, too.

"Food is the most primitive form of comfort."
—Sheilah Graham, British-American gossip columnist and mistress to F. Scott Fitzgerald

1 (14.5-ounce) package gingerbread mix, plus ingredients to make it
1 (3-ounce) package lemon gelatin
$^{1}/_{2}$ cup water
$^{1}/_{2}$ cup orange juice
$^{1}/_{2}$ cup lemon rum
$^{1}/_{4}$ cup Southern Comfort
$^{1}/_{8}$ cup Grand Marnier
$^{1}/_{8}$ cup Rose's Sweetened Lime Juice
1 (7-ounce) can whipped cream (optional)

In an 8 by 8-inch or 9 by 9-inch pan, make and bake the gingerbread as directed on the mix's package. Let the gingerbread cool completely in the pan.

Place the gelatin in a heat-resistant bowl. Combine the water and orange juice and bring to a boil. Pour the liquid over the gelatin and mix well. Add the lemon rum, Southern Comfort, Grand Marnier, and Rose's Sweetened Lime Juice, mixing well. Let the mixture cool for 10 minutes.

While the gelatin is cooling, carefully poke holes in the cake with a fork. Try not to puncture the bottom of the cake but don't worry if you do. Have fun! Poke a lot of holes. Pour $1^{1}/_{2}$ cups of the mixture very slowly over cake. The mixture will drain into the holes. Cover the cake and refrigerate it for at least 4 hours and up to 1 day.

Distribute the remaining jiggelo mixture among 10 disposable 1-ounce cups. Chill in the refrigerator until firm, 2 to 4 hours.

Serve the cake cold and garnish with whipped cream. The cake will keep in the refrigerator for 3 days.

Serves 8 and makes 4 to 6 extra jiggelos

Chocolate-Raspberry Party Poke Cake

Divine. Two of the most wickedly scrumptious tastes on earth meet in one insanely moist, outrageously intense cake. This delight is reason enough to party—a jiggelo cake that will rock everyone's paradigm!

"Look, there's no metaphysics on earth like chocolates."
—Fernando Pessoa, Modernist Portuguese poet

1 (18.25-ounce) chocolate cake mix, plus the ingredients to make it
1 (3-ounce) package raspberry gelatin
1 cup water
$\frac{1}{2}$ cup raspberry vodka or other berry vodka
$\frac{1}{3}$ cup crème de cacao
2 tablespoons Chambord
1 (7-ounce) can whipped cream (optional)
1 pint fresh raspberries (optional)

In a 9 by 13-inch pan, make and bake the chocolate cake as directed on the cake's package. Let the cake cool completely in the pan.

Place the gelatin in a heat-resistant bowl. Bring the water to a boil. Pour the water over the gelatin, stirring until dissolved. Add the raspberry vodka, crème de cacao, and Chambord, mixing well. Let the mixture cool for 10 minutes.

While the mixture is cooling, carefully poke holes in the cake with a fork. Try not to puncture the bottom of the cake but don't worry if you do. Have fun! Poke a lot of holes. Very slowly pour the mixture over the cake. The mixture will drain into the holes. Cover the cake and refrigerate for at least 4 hours and up to 1 day. Serve the cake cold. Garnish with whipped cream and fresh raspberries. The cake will keep covered in the refrigerator for up to 3 days.

Serves 12

Jiggelo Jubilations

Events large and small call for jiggelos. You know they add to the festivities at birthday parties, holidays, wedding showers, and landmark celebrations. The following is an abbreviated list of appropriate jiggelos for less traditional occasions. The world is your oyster.

Random Events

Calendar Events

January 13: Charles Nelson Reilly's birthday
ISO Gainful Employment, page 20
ISO Alternatives, page 26

February: National Snack Food Month
Twinkle Dare, page 73
Crazy Ho, page 78
Rapture, page 62

February 4: Anniversary of Patty Hearst's Abduction
Cult of Minthe, page 72
Exile, page 31
ISO Happy Endings, page 27

The first week in March: National Procrastination Week
Pending

The second week in April: National Lingerie Week
Cosmo Royale, page 30
Spice, Spice Baby, page 40
Cordial Rose, page 76

May's Full Moon: Frog's Return Moon
ISO Happy Endings, page 27
Tree Hugger Smoothie, page 65

June 24: National Dryer Lint Appreciation Day
Cram, page 14
Crazy Ho, page 78
Miraculous Conception, page 80

July: National Hot Dog Month
Skid Marks, page 40
Orangerie, page 54
Martinique Mojo, page 56

August 27: Anniversary of Pee-Wee Herman's arrest
Peter Blow, page 11
ISO Alternatives, page 26

The third week in September: National Singles Week
Need, page 12
ISO Ms. Right, page 24
ISO Mr. Right, page 25
ISO Happy Endings, page 27

September 9: Hugh Grant's birthday
Peter Blow, page 11
Bloody Good, page 32
Paternity Sample, page 60

The fourth week in October: National Consumers Week
Four batches of Need, page 12

November: National Novel Writing Month
Alliteration, page 10
The Hem, page 36
ISO Happy Endings, page 27

December 5: Anniversary of the repeal of prohibition
Jungle Juice, page 13
ISO Mr. Right, page 25
Jacks over 7s, page 35

Resources

One-ounce disposable soufflé cups

Most restaurant supply stores and some large party supply stores carry the plastic 1-ounce disposable soufflé cups we recommend. They are affordable and lids are available but not necessary. These online and phone sources will help:

- www.acemart.com
- www.fultonparty.com
- www.gfs.com (Find your local Gordon Food Service location or phone number.)

Chocolate cups

You may be able to find chocolate soufflé cups at a gourmet food store. Many online cooking sites have recipes and directions for making your own chocolate cups. You may order chocolate cups online or by phone but avoid shipment during very hot months because cups may melt. Some resources for ordering chocolate cups are:

- www.ambassadorfoods.com/ChocolateCups.html (Ambassador Fine Foods has an amazing assortment of sizes, shapes, and kinds of chocolate cups, using good quality Callebaut chocolate. These products are available by phone ordering only. You can view their line of chocolate containers and find their phone numbers on their website.)
- www.happycookers.com
- www.thechocolateshoppe.com
- www.gogourmetfood.com

Vegetarian gelatin

Many health food stores carry Hain SuperFruits Dessert Mixes. They come in strawberry, orange, raspberry, and cherry. SuperFruits can also be ordered online at:

- www.vegangoods.com
- www.shopnatural.com

Liquor Index

Acknowledgements

Jiggelo was conceived during a lively evening of safe but inventive imbibing. It began with a catfish dinner at Frank and Mary's in Pittsboro, Indiana, and ended with lots of jiggelo speculation.

A special thank-you to Ian Forbes, a gelatin shot co-conspirator in the pre-jiggelo days. Sincere thanks to Steve Paddack for his unending support, love, and creative presence. Heart-felt gratitude to Wayne Hobson for beautiful listening, thoughtful readings, and pedicure admiration.

To our supportive friends, family, and neighbors in Indiana, Maine, California, and Connecticut: thank you for listening, celebrating, and all that jiggelo taste testing. We're very sorry about the failed dayglow licorice recipe. Thanks to Amy, Angel, B. A., Brett, Brian, Bridget, Carrie, Charmwood's Posse, Chris, the Coveside Restaurant crew, Dad, Daniel, Eliza, the exiled Scotsman, the General, Greg, HDFC, J&J, Jamie, Jen, Joe, Karen, Karon, Krista, Kyle, Lance, Leila, Lisa, Lucy, Melanie, Meredith, Mike, Mom, Moukie, Nina, Peggy, Rich, Rick, Rob, Roger, Shawn, Sherri, the Smith family, Space Pants, Ted, and Worm.

Numerous people graciously opened their photo and memorabilia collections to us. These images and artifacts have enriched the visual presence of *Jiggelo*. Many thanks to Sandra McCandless and Frederick Nove (page 38), Janet Voigt (pages 6, 48, and 70), Angela Breidenbach (pages 24 and 25), John Ibson (page 26), and James Lamkin. We'd like to thank every person whose spirited images are depicted here. Most of you are unknown to us, but the joyfulness of your images spoke to us of the pleasures of life.

Thank you to our Ten Speed editors, Windy Ferges and Brie Mazurek. Their support of our vision and their jiggelosity made working with them a pleasure.

Life would have been bleak without our trusty pizza places for sustenance: (Circle City Pizza in Indianapolis, Indiana; Rosario's in New Harbor, Maine; and BJ's in Brea, California).

About the Authors

Mary Breidenbach (design) is an Indianapolis-based freelance graphic designer. When she's not in front of her computer, she volunteers at Do It, where she instructs the hesitant in jiggelo consuming techniques. She's known to break into spontaneous Oakenfold dancing.

Barrett J. Calhoon (recipes and jiggelo photography) is an Indianapolis resident struggling to wean himself from his addiction to higher education and into a journey in new media and technology. An aficionado of contemporary culture, Barrett throws legendary parties that are studies in creative imbibing.

Sharon L. Calhoon (text) is an award-winning freelance writer whose articles on culture and the arts have appeared in numerous magazines and newspapers. She is bi-coastal, residing in mid-coast Maine and Orange County, California, and has served jiggelos to lobstermen, professors, musicians, firemen, chefs, artists, and the unemployed.